HIP-HOP
Biographies

DATE DUE	
	PRINTED IN U.S.A.

SADDLEBACK
PUBLISHING

Chris Brown	Pitbull
Drake	Rihanna
50 Cent	Usher
Jay-Z	Lil Wayne
Nicki Minaj	Kanye West

SADDLEBACK
PUBLISHING
www.sdlback.com

ISBN-13: 978-162250-008-6
ISBN-10: 1-62250-008-3
eBook: 978-1-61247-689-6

Printed in Guangzhou, China
NOR/1012/CA21201318
16 15 14 13 12   1 2 3 4 5

Table of Contents

Timeline

1975: Curtis Jackson III, now known as 50 Cent, is born on July 6.

1983: 50 Cent's mother is murdered.

1986: 50 Cent becomes friends with *drug dealer* Sincere.

1987: 50 Cent starts selling drugs.

1991: 50 Cent arrested for the first time.

1994: 50 Cent sent to Monterey Shock Incarceration.

1996: 50 Cent meets Run-D.M.C.'s Jam Master Jay.

1997: 50 Cent's son, Marquise, is born.

1999: 50 Cent signs recording *contract* with Columbia Records. 50 Cent records song "How to Rob" on his own when Columbia Records is slow to promote him.

2000: 50 Cent stabbed in March, and then shot two months later. 50 Cent starts recording *mixtapes* to promote his music.

2002: 50 Cent signs record deal with Eminem and Dr. Dre.

2003: 50 Cent releases album *Get Rich or Die Tryin'.*

50 Cent wins two MTV Video Music Awards and two American Music Awards.

50 Cent starts G-Unit Records.

2004: 50 Cent becomes a co-owner of company that makes Vitaminwater.

2005: 50 Cent releases second album, *The Massacre.*

50 Cent appears in movie *Get Rich or Die Tryin'.*

2007: 50 Cent starts his own line of books, G-Unit Books.

50 Cent releases third album, *Curtis.*

50 Cent earns $100 million when Coca-Cola buys Vitaminwater.

2010: 50 Cent wins a Grammy Award for a song he recorded with Eminem and Dr. Dre.

2009: 50 Cent releases fourth album, *Before I Self Destruct.*

2012: 50 Cent releases fifth album, *Five (Murder by Numbers).*

5

Young Life

The world knows 50 Cent as a hip-hop artist and movie star. He has won dozens of awards and made millions of dollars. He works to end hunger around the world. But 50 Cent, also known as Fiddy, grew up living a very different life. Back then, people called him Boo-Boo.

Curtis James Jackson III was born on July 6, 1975, in Queens, New York. His mother, Sabrina, was fifteen years old at the time. She named him after her father. But Sabrina and everyone else called her son Boo-Boo.

After Boo-Boo was born, Sabrina moved out of her parents' home but often left her son with them. She did not come around often. When she did, she often had a gift for Boo-Boo. She gave clothes, toys, and cash to make up for not being there as he grew up. "Every visit was like Christmas," Boo-Boo said.

Nobody talked about how Sabrina got the money to buy Boo-Boo's gifts. She did not finish high school. But she got a place to live and new car. Finally, when Boo-Boo was seven years old, he saw his mother at work. She was a drug dealer.

Boo-Boo grew up in Queens, New York, in a neighborhood called South Jamaica. It was a rough neighborhood.

In 1983 his grandmother sat him down to talk. She sadly told him that Sabrina would never pick him up again. She did not say it, but Boo-Boo knew. His mother was dead. He was just eight years old. Years later, he learned what happened. Someone put something in Sabrina's drink that knocked her out. Then the gas was turned on in her home with all of the doors and windows closed. The gas killed Sabrina. The police never found out who murdered her.

Losing his mother was very hard for Boo-Boo. He was angry and sad. He acted out. He was rude in class and at home. If someone wanted him to do something, he would do something different instead. He got into a lot of trouble.

Boo-Boo's grandmother and grandfather had eight of their own kids at home. They had Boo-Boo too. That meant eleven people shared their small home.

Boo-Boo was the youngest of the family. His uncles gave him the clothes that were too small for them. Boo-Boo was embarrassed to wear old, worn-out clothing. But he also knew that there was no money to spend on him.

Boo-Boo watched the other kids and teens in the neighborhood. When he saw someone in a cool sweat suit, he would tell people, "I'm getting those." If someone drove by in a fancy car, he said, "That will be my car." He wanted the brand-name shoes and jewelry that other kids had.

Sincere was a teenager who lived in the same neighborhood. He saw that Boo-Boo needed clothes and shoes. Sincere would take Boo-Boo shopping and buy new clothes and shoes. Boo-Boo was happy to dress like he had money.

Boo-Boo wanted to wear track suits, sneakers, and big gold jewelry.

The only problem was his grandmother. She would not let Boo-Boo keep the clothes that Sincere bought. Boo-Boo's aunts and uncles would be *jealous* of his fancy clothes too. So he hid the clothes and shoes at a friend's house. He would leave for school early and head to the friend's house instead. He could change into his nice clothes.

Drugs were very common in South Jamaica, Queens. Boo-Boo's aunts and uncles used *cocaine*. His uncle Harold was selling it. His uncle Trevor was dealing drugs too. The people with money were selling drugs. To Boo-Boo, being around drugs was normal. And selling drugs looked like the way to make easy cash.

Uncle Harold made enough money to buy a house in Miami. Uncle Trevor replaced Boo-Boo's grandmother's old, broken-down car. Now she was driving a brand-new Mercedes-Benz. Sincere had more money than he needed. This made selling drugs look like a great job.

Then Boo-Boo saw the dangers in selling drugs. People talked about the money Sincere was making. Sincere's grandfather was kidnapped. The kidnappers wanted Sincere's money. When they got it, they shot the grandfather anyway.

Boo-Boo's cousin Brian was dealing drugs too. Thieves tried to break into his house. Brian's mother blocked the door, and the thieves shot her in the head. Drugs made the neighborhood dangerous. People became targets because they were selling. Other people got hurt for being in the wrong place at the wrong time.

Officer Edward Byrne was in his patrol car in Boo-Boo's neighborhood when someone shot him five times. The New York Police Department acted quickly. They formed a Tactical Narcotics Team to try to stop the drug sales. They sent dealers to jail.

The government started a program, the War on Drugs. The police told kids to "Just Say No." New laws put drug dealers in prison for many years. But it did not stop the drugs. The drug dealers just moved to places where police could not see them. Over time, the drugs and the danger returned.

Officer Byrne's murder caused the police to crack down on drug crimes.

Dealing Drugs

Boo-Boo's aunts and uncles would throw parties at home. Friends would come over, listen to music, and use cocaine. If they ran out, his uncles or aunts would send Boo-Boo down to Sincere or his cousin Brian to get more. Brian was rude to Boo-Boo, but Sincere was friendly. Sincere would talk to Boo-Boo and help him when he needed it. So Boo-Boo only bought his family's drugs from Sincere.

One day, Sincere explained that he could not keep buying Boo-Boo clothes and shoes. He wanted Boo-Boo to learn how to take care of himself. So he gave Boo-Boo cocaine and told him to sell it to his uncles and aunts. Boo-Boo could sell it for $125, give Sincere $100, and keep the rest. At age eleven, Boo-Boo became a drug dealer.

At first, Boo-Boo's family did not know he was selling drugs. When someone gave Boo-Boo money to buy drugs, he took some from his closet. Then he walked around the block, pretending to go to Sincere's house. He came back and handed them the drugs. But after a while, Boo-Boo wanted to make more money than just from his family. So he would sell drugs in the neighborhood after school. His grandparents had no idea what he was doing. They thought he was hanging out with friends or playing.

Boo-Boo started making enough money to buy food after school. He could buy his own clothes and shoes. Police officers were on the streets looking for people with drugs. But Boo-Boo kept his drugs hidden. He was careful to sell his drugs where the police could not see him.

Boo-Boo started dealing drugs at age eleven.

Boo-Boo made more money making crack for other dealers than selling on the streets. He bought cocaine from Sincere. He cooked it into crack in Sincere's or Brian's kitchen. Then he sold it to dealers in the neighborhood. It was less work than selling the drugs himself. It also made more money because people were buying a lot more crack than cocaine.

Boo-Boo kept his drugs in his bedroom. When people called him to buy the drugs, he would grab what he needed from his closet. He knew not to carry any extra drugs. He sold what he had as quickly as possible. If he was caught with any of the drugs, he could go to jail.

Once, a dealer accused Boo-Boo of selling him less than he paid for. Boo-Boo thought the dealer was trying to scare him. Boo-Boo was still in junior high school. He was younger and smaller than his adult customers. So Boo-Boo acted tough. He pretended he had a gun in his pocket and scared his customer away.

At home, Boo-Boo found his uncle in his room. He was stealing drugs from Boo-Boo. This meant that Boo-Boo had been selling smaller packages of drugs and charging more for them. Boo-Boo would be in big trouble with his customers.

Angry customers could be dangerous to Boo-Boo. He started going to a gym to learn to box. Boo-Boo had a talent for boxing. He would learn at the gym and practice on the streets. He would fight anyone who made him angry. Soon people knew not to mess with him.

Boo-Boo was still making and selling crack in high school. The school had problems with drugs and violence, so students had to go through a metal detector. Security guards would search the kids who looked like they had something to hide. One day Boo-Boo was pulled aside. When the guard checked his shoes, he found some crack. Boo-Boo forgot to put the drugs in his closet. He was suspended from school.

Boo-Boo's grandparents were very upset. They were also worried that Boo-Boo was using drugs. Boo-Boo explained that he sold drugs, but he never used them. His grandmother told Boo-Boo how sorry she was. She thought she should have done more to protect him.

Then Boo-Boo was caught selling drugs. Because he was young, he went to a rehab program. He lived with other people who had been arrested for drug crimes. They had to go to classes and follow strict rules. Boo-Boo hated it, but he followed the rules so he could go home as soon as possible.

When he came home from rehab, Boo-Boo started selling drugs again. In 1994 the police came to his home. They found $15,000 and drugs. He could have gone to jail

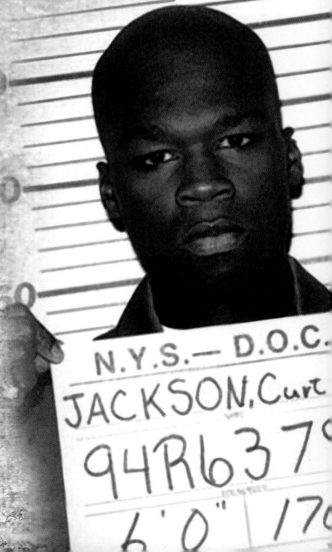

N.Y.S.— D.O.C.
JACKSON, Curt
94R637
6'0" 17

for years. Instead, he was given the chance to go to Monterey Shock Incarceration for six months. Shock was like *boot camp*. Boo-Boo had to wake up before dawn, run, chop trees, and anything else he was told to do. He also earned his high school *diploma* there.

Went he left Shock, Boo-Boo still sold drugs. But he knew he would get caught again. His *probation officer* suggested he start to *rap*. So he started writing music.

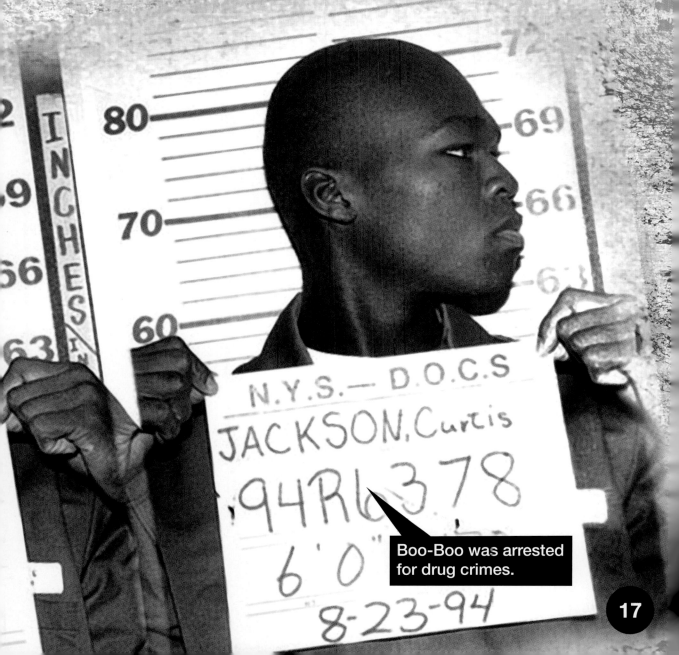

Boo-Boo was arrested for drug crimes.

Making Music

Jam Master Jay was in the hit hip-hop group Run-D.M.C. He was a talented musician. He was also a great DJ. He worked in New York City clubs, mixing music. Jay started his own record company after Run-D.M.C. became famous.

Boo-Boo met Jam Master Jay at a dance club in 1996. The DJ found out that he was trying to get out of the drug business. Jay also heard that Boo-Boo could write and rap. The DJ gave Boo-Boo a CD and asked him to write words for the music on it. Boo-Boo wrote lyrics and gave them to Jay. In 1997 Boo-Boo signed a deal with Jay's record company.

The name Boo-Boo was a problem, though. It did not sound right for a serious rapper. So Boo-Boo came up with a new name, 50 Cent, or Fiddy. There was a robber in Brooklyn who

Run-D.M.C.'s Jam Master Jay gave 50 Cent his first break.

called himself 50 Cent. Calling himself by this name would make Boo-Boo sound tough. The name 50 Cent also reminded Boo-Boo of change. Switching from drugs to hip-hop would be a big change.

Fiddy had good reasons not to sell drugs anymore. Jam Master Jay would not let 50 Cent deal drugs while he had the recording contract. And in 1997, 50 Cent's girlfriend gave birth to their son, Marquise. Fiddy did not want to risk hurting his new family. He put all of his energy into making music.

Working with Jam Master Jay helped 50 Cent understand the music business. At first, Fiddy did not make records, but he wrote music. Jay sold the songs to other artists. So people like Jay-Z recorded 50 Cent's songs. Fiddy made a little money this way. But he wanted the money that came with selling hit records.

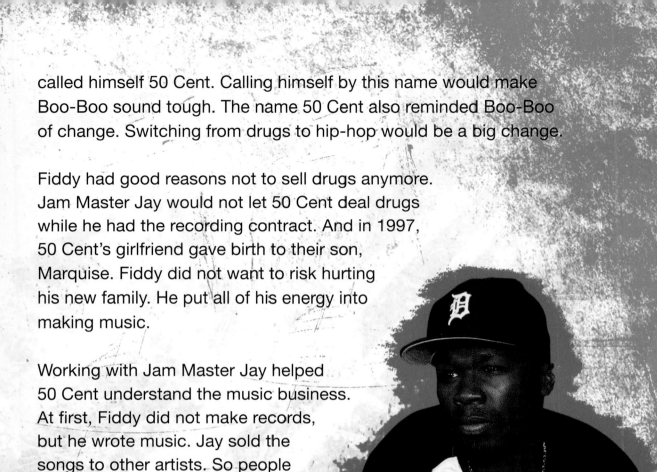

Fiddy stopped selling drugs when he became a father.

19

Fiddy thought that if he made an album, he would start making more money. One day he saw a producer with Columbia Records at a barbershop. Columbia Records was a much bigger company. They had hip-hop artists like LL Cool J and Public Enemy. So 50 Cent walked up to the producer and gave him a tape of his music. The producer called at two o'clock the next morning. He offered 50 Cent a record deal.

The only problem was that 50 Cent had a contract with Jam Master Jay. Fiddy took the money from Columbia and gave it to Jay. In return, Jay let him out of the contract.

Columbia had 50 Cent recording right away. In two weeks, he had a demo to send to radio stations and clubs. But Columbia did not send out the record to anybody for eight months. So 50 Cent took action.

The Wu-Tang Clan rapped about 50 Cent, helping him become famous.

Fiddy recorded a new song that he wrote, "How to Rob." He sang about robbing famous black celebrities like Will Smith, Mike Tyson, and Whitney Houston. He wrote it as a joke. He also repeated his name throughout the song. This would help people know who he was. He did not wait for Columbia to send out the record. He made his own copies and gave them to DJs around New York.

The song became a hit. Some celebrities were angry that this unknown rapper made fun of them. Others thought it was funny. Rappers answered him back in their songs. Hearing groups like Wu-Tang Clan rap his name made 50 Cent even more popular.

One rapper who did not like "How to Rob" was Ja Rule. Ja was a rapper from Queens, like 50 Cent. After "How to Rob" came out, a friend of 50 Cent's actually robbed Ja Rule. Ja thought Fiddy was partly to blame for his being robbed. Ja started to say bad things about 50 Cent, saying he could not rap.

The feud was on. Fiddy would rap insults about Ja Rule and the group he performed with, Murder Inc. Ja would rap insults back toward 50 Cent. If they ran into each other on the street or at a show, they would fight.

In March 2000, 50 Cent was recording songs at the Hit Factory studio in New York. Ja Rule was recording in another room at the same studio. When he heard 50 Cent was there, Ja Rule and his friends snuck into 50 Cent's studio. They turned out the lights and then beat up 50 Cent. When the fight was over and Fiddy turned on the lights, he saw he had been stabbed. Fortunately, 50 Cent recovered quickly.

Two months later, 50 Cent was visiting his grandmother's house. His son was there too. Fiddy climbed into the back of a friend's car. Another car pulled up next to 50 Cent. Someone in the other car shot Fiddy nine times. Fiddy's friend rushed him to the hospital. The shooter was never caught.

Fiddy was shot in his arm, leg, and face. One of the bullets was in 50 Cent's tongue. The doctors wanted to remove the bullet, but it might ruin his speech. Fiddy's grandmother knew he wanted to perform. So she would not allow the surgery. He survived, but part of a bullet is still in his tongue today.

Ja Rule and 50 Cent had a long-running feud.

Starting Over

Fiddy stayed in the hospital for thirteen days. He refused to see most visitors. Fiddy was afraid that people would think he was weak. When he left the hospital, 50 Cent moved out of town. He did not want anyone to see him until he was well again.

Because of the gunshot to his face, 50 Cent's jaw was wired shut. This injury took six weeks to heal. He could only drink, not eat. So he lost a lot of weight. He could not walk. One of the bullets broke the bone in his hip. As he healed, he was able to start walking. Then he rode a bike to help build his muscles. Fiddy worked out in the gym as often as possible to regain his strength. It took over a year for him to make a full recovery.

Finally, 50 Cent was ready to go back to recording. But Columbia was no longer interested in working with him. They were scared of the violence that followed him. They dropped him from his contract. No other record company wanted to deal with him.

Fiddy still had enemies from his days selling drugs. He also had angered people in the music business like Ja Rule. So Fiddy wore a *bulletproof vest* wherever he went. He carried a gun.

People remembered that 50 Cent was a great songwriter. So instead of giving him work as a rapper, they offered him work writing. Sean "Diddy" Combs offered to hire 50 Cent as a songwriter. Fiddy showed up with his bulletproof vest and gun. Diddy said that he did not want the drama. He turned 50 Cent away.

Fiddy's face is scarred from his shooting.

Success!

Two years of hard work changed everything for 50 Cent. In 2000 no record company would touch him. Now in 2002 they were fighting to get him to record for them. Fiddy still wore his bulletproof vest. Before, the record companies did not want to deal with someone with violent enemies. But now that 50 Cent was so popular, they did not care.

Fiddy looked at the different contracts very carefully. Most of the companies offered a lot of money. But 50 Cent wanted to work with people who loved hip-hop. One night, he got a call from a lawyer. The man said that the hip-hop artists Eminem and Dr. Dre wanted to talk to him. The hip-hop artists were hugely popular. They also had their own small record company.

Eminem and Dr. Dre asked 50 Cent to fly to Los Angeles the next morning. Fiddy almost missed his flight. As he went through security, the agents noticed his bulletproof vest. They pulled him aside and questioned him. Finally, one of the agents recognized him and let him go.

When 50 Cent got to Los Angeles, he went to a movie set. Eminem was making a movie called *8 Mile*. The men met and agreed to a contract. Eminem also asked 50 Cent to record a song for the movie soundtrack. Eminem told Fiddy that he was going to be a big star.

He was right. Eminem used the song "Wangsta" in the *8 Mile* movie soundtrack. The song became a huge hit. Hip-hop fans became even more excited about 50 Cent's music.

Eminem (left) and Dr. Dre (right) wanted to make 50 Cent a star.

With the help of Enimem and Dr. Dre, 50 Cent was ready to release his first album. Record companies want their albums to sell very well. One way they get customers excited is to release lead singles. A single is a song from the album. A lead single comes out before the album is out. That way, people hear the song and hopefully like it. With a hit lead single, more customers will buy the whole album.

Fiddy's lead single was "In da Club." The song was released in January 2003. Music critics liked it, and radio stations played it. People across the country danced to the song in clubs. They also sang along with the words.

The song was a huge hit. The album, *Get Rich or Die Tryin'*, was released a few weeks later. It sold 800,000 records the first week. The album was a top seller the same week. By the end of the year, it sold over 12 million copies. Other hip-hop stars performed with Fiddy, including Snoop Dogg, Eminem, and Dr. Dre. He also rapped with the rest of G-Unit on one of his songs.

Fiddy's album got three Grammy nominations. He also won the MTV Video Award for Best Rap Video as well as Best New Artist. Two years later, 50 Cent released his second album, *The Massacre*. It also earned Grammy nominations and great sales.

Fiddy's musical career was finally taking off. But at the same time, his personal life was suffering. He and his girlfriend broke up. This meant that he would not be able to see his son as often.

MTV named 50 Cent the Best New Artist in 2003.

Movies and More Music

After his first album took off, 50 Cent made another deal with Eminem and Dr. Dre. They formed a new record label just for 50 Cent. He called the label G-Unit Records. G-Unit recorded on the label. Fiddy also signed new artist Young Buck.

Next, 50 Cent made a deal with Reebok. Sneakers were still part of hip-hop style. Reebok made sneakers that 50 Cent put his logo on called G-Force. The sneakers sold out in weeks.

Fiddy was showing that he could be successful in music and business. He was finally making more money in music than in the drug business. But people still criticized him. Some rappers said that he was not in touch with street life anymore. Others said that he was trying to get on *pop* radio. They felt 50 Cent's music was not tough enough.

One person who went after 50 Cent was rapper The Game. Eminem and Dr. Dre planned on working with The Game, but then they found 50 Cent. The Game's record was put on hold. Fiddy made The Game part of G-Unit and helped him put out his first record. But the two rappers became angry with each other. Fiddy fired The Game from G-Unit on the air during a radio show. From then on, The Game bad-mouthed 50 Cent. Fiddy insulted The Game right back.

Fiddy had a sneaker with Reebok called the G-Force.

The Game sang about 50 Cent in a mixtape called "Stop Snitchin, Stop Lyin." Fiddy made fun of The Game in his song "Not Rich, Still Lyin." G-Unit members attacked The Game in their music. His friends attacked right back in their songs. The feud led to dozens of *diss* records.

Fiddy was inspired by Eminem's movie. The movie *8 Mile* was similar to Eminem's life story. The movie was very successful. The soundtrack sold over three million copies. Eminem won an Academy Award for Best Original Song. Fiddy hoped to have similar success, so he turned his story into a movie.

A screenwriter had 50 Cent tell his life story. The writer used the stories from 50 Cent's life to write a movie. Some of the movie was exactly what happened to Fiddy. Other parts the writer made up to make the movie more exciting or interesting. The movies title was *Get Rich or Die Tryin',* just like Fiddy's first album.

Fiddy played the main character, Marcus. Well-known actors Terrence Howard and Viola Davis starred in the movie with him. The director was Jim Sheridan. He'd been nominated for Academy Awards six times before.

Even with well-known stars and a successful director, the movie was not a hit. Critics were not impressed with how the story was told. The film made only a little bit more money than it cost to make it. Terrence Howard won an award for Best Actor in the film from Black Entertainment Television. The Teen Choice Awards nominated 50 Cent for Choice Breakout (Male) actor. But the movie was nowhere near the success that *8 Mile* was.

Although the soundtrack had the same name as 50 Cent's earlier album, the songs on the soundtrack were completely different. Fiddy had rappers from G-Force Records singing many of the songs. Three of the songs made in onto the *Billboard* Hot 100 chart.

Fiddy starred in the movie *Get Rich or Die Tryin'*.

Kanye West and 50 Cent had a challenge to see who could sell the most albums.

Fiddy went back to making music. His next album, *Curtis*, was scheduled to be released on September 11, 2007. Hip-hop artist Kanye West had an album, *Graduation*, coming out a week later. When he found out that 50 Cent's album was coming out only a week earlier, Kanye moved the date to the same day. Kanye did not say so, but it was a challenge. Who would sell more records?

Fiddy understood that this was a challenge too. He did not sit back and wait to see what happened. Instead, he upped the challenge. He announced that if he did not sell more records than Kanye the week the album was released, he would stop writing music.

Hip-hop fans were thrilled with the challenge. Kanye and 50 Cent were invited to television and radio shows. The music magazine *Rolling Stone* put Kanye and 50 Cent on the cover and ran a story about them.

For 50 Cent, *Curtis* would be different from his other records. Instead of working with people only from his record company, he sang with many other artists. Justin Timberlake, Mary J. Blige, and Robin Thicke all appeared on the album. Fiddy felt that working with new artists was a way to experiment with his sound.

September 11 came, and both albums were released. At the end of the week, Kanye sold 957,000 albums and landed at the top of *Billboard*'s album chart. *Curtis* sold 691,000 copies. Kanye won the battle. But together, the two artists created the best-selling week in history for hip-hop music.

And 50 Cent did not stop writing music.

Growing His Empire

Even though the movie *Get Rich or Die Tryin'* did not do as well as he had hoped, 50 Cent did not stop acting. He appeared in over a dozen movies. He also was a guest star in the television shows *Entourage* and *The Simpsons*. The acting experience led 50 Cent to writing for movies.

Fiddy wrote the movies *Gun* and *All Things Fall Apart*. He starred in both movies and was able to sign major stars to work with him. Neither movie won any awards, but *All Things Fall Apart* received good reviews.

The writing did not stop there. In the book *From Pieces to Weight*, 50 Cent wrote his life story. Next, 50 Cent wrote for teens. *The Playground* tells the story of a bully named Butterball, who is thirteen years old. Writing the book from the bully's perspective was a new way to talk about the problem. Fiddy hoped to stop bullying by reaching the kids doing it.

Fiddy also released a series of books. The books were based on living in cities and dealing with drugs and crime. The G-Unit series were written by many authors. But by adding his name to the books, they were successful.

And the books kept coming. Years earlier, 50 Cent read the book *The 48 Laws of Power* by Robert Greene. The book described how to use power to succeed in business. Fiddy was a big fan of Greene's book. In 2009 they worked together to write *The 50th Law.* The book gives examples and advice on being fearless. The book was such a hit that a comic book version of it followed.

Fiddy has a line of books called the G-Unit series.

G Unit

Fiddy made millions of dollars when he sold his part of the Vitaminwater company.

Reading books like *The 48 Laws of Power* helped 50 Cent understand business and leadership. With that information, he started investing in more companies. He became a part owner of Vitaminwater because he believed in it. He liked that it was a healthier choice than sodas and sweet sports drinks. When Coca-Cola bought the company, he made $100 million.

Fiddy also launched a clothing brand, G-Unit Clothing. The company lasted for a few years but eventually closed down. G-Unit Clothing sold $75 million in clothes while they were in business.

People in many different businesses wanted to get into the popularity of hip-hop. The makers of *Grand Theft Auto: San Andreas* asked 50 Cent to act as the voice of the main character. Fiddy would only play himself—not another character. So *50 Cent: Bulletproof* was developed just for him. Eminem, Dr. Dre, and artists from G-Unit acted as other voices in the game. *Blood on the Sand* was the sequel to *Bulletproof*.

Fiddy worked with other companies as well. He continued with his line of Reebok sneakers. Pontiac paid 50 Cent to include some of their cars in a music video. In a short time, 50 Cent was named one of hip-hop's "Cash Kings." In other words, he became one of the top five richest hip-hop artists.

Fame and fortune gave 50 Cent a way to meet famous women. He dated actress Vivica A. Fox when he was twenty-seven and she was thirty-nine. He has had an on-and-off relationship with singer Ciara. He also dated actress and talk-show host Chelsea Handler.

As a kid, Boo-Boo used drug money for shoes and clothes. As an adult, 50 Cent uses his music and businesses to help others.

After his album *Get Rich or Die Tryin'*, 50 Cent formed the G-Unity Foundation. The organization helps people go to college. It gives money to groups helping low-income neighborhoods. It also pays for after-school activities to keep kids off the streets.

Fiddy owns part of an energy drink company. He and his partner agreed to give back money as their business succeeds. So for every drink they sell, the company buys a meal for a starving child in Africa. This program has paid for over three million meals so far. He traveled to Africa to help promote the program and meet the kids in need.

He was so successful using energy drinks to feed starving children that he decided he could feed kids at home too. He has his own brand of headphones. With every pair sold, 50 Cent pays for 250 meals for children here in the United States. His giving has been so successful, Fiddy has started pushing for other companies to give money to charities too.

Fiddy helps raise money to feed children around the world.

Rapper 50 Cent has lived a life of crime and of success. He also has many critics. Some of his songs are about drugs and violence. He has been arrested. But he also turned his life around. Does he think he is a role model for his young fans?

He talks about being a role model in the book about his life. "I don't think it makes me a role model. I think it makes me inspiring. 'Cos I'm from the bottom I think they look at me and go 'Well, if he made it, I can make it.'"

Photo Credits